The Thing About Dairy Farmers

Also by Natasha Metzler

Pain Redeemed: when our deepest sorrows meet God

The Thing About Dairy Farmers

WIT AND HUMOR FROM A FARMER'S WIFE

———————— ~ ————————

Natasha Metzler

ISBN: 1493567187
ISBN-13: 978-1493567188

The Thing About Dairy Farmers
Published by Natasha Metzler
3837 State Rt. 177
Lowville, NY 13367

Cover design by Natasha Metzler

Names have been changed to protect the identity of the farmers. If you think I'm talking about you, well, you're probably correct.

All Scripture quotations taken from THE HOLY BIBLE, NEW INTERNATIONAL VERSION®, NIV® Copyright © 1973, 1978, 1984, 2011 by Biblica, Inc.® Used by permission. All rights reserved worldwide.

All photographs © 2013 Natasha Metzler

All artwork © 2013 Brianna Siegrist

Farmland © 2012 Brianna Siegrist, used with permission

Praise for *The Thing About Dairy Farmers*

"Natasha's book had me in fits of laughter and brought to mind my own farm stories from growing up. – Jessica White, *mama to four little ones with plenty of "farm-time" under her belt*

"I started reading *The Thing About Dairy Farmers* on a trip from New York to Alabama. My sister-in-law and I both loved it and were laughing right out loud at the hilarious stories." – Trina Holden, *raw-milk-loving-mama who spent her teenage years on a homestead in Upstate New York*

"*The Thing About Dairy Farmers* brings you so up close and personal to dairy farming, you can hear the streams of milk and smell the manure. Whether you're in farming or just an interested onlooker, you'll laugh until you cry over these personal anecdotes from a dairy farmer's wife." – Gretchen Louise, *the wife of a farmer who says he's never going to be a dairy farmer*

Natasha Metzler

Dedicated To
the dairy farmers of Lewis County

Natasha Metzler

contents

Natasha Metzler

Introduction

I still remember the first cow I ever milked. She was affectionately called "19" and was a big black cow with a deep hanging udder and a pretty face.

I carefully placed the milking unit on her while leaning as far away from her feet as possible.

Larry, the man who sold us the cows, stood behind me and said in a low drawl, "Now girly, if a cow is gonna kick ya, I guarantee you'll want to be closer to her feet rather than far away. Less room to gain momentum, you see."

Turns out he was exactly right.

The worst kick I ever sustained came from a feisty little heifer, "36." She was part Ayrshire, part Holstein, and 100% stubborn. She had a sore teat and a sour mood that morning so when I leaned in to wash her udder, a flying hoof sent me sprawling across the barn floor.

I had been pretty close, practically underneath her, so while my balance had been lost the pain was still minimal.

I stood up, dusted myself off and turned to pick up the towel I had dropped, completely forgetting to watch where I was standing. When the next kick hit my upper thigh, it felt as though someone had imprinted my leg with a hoof-shaped branding iron.

I learned something that day. Farmers have a higher level of know-how than most anyone else in the world. It's a certain breed of smarts that can't be taught in schools. It can only be earned through blood and sweat and impressive black and blue marks.

It's not about being tough, anyone can be tough. It's not about being intelligent, anyone can read a book.

It's about being smart. And you can only learn about being smart by being dumb. I know. I got the hoof print on my thigh to prove it.

The Thing About Dairy Farmers

You might be a dairy farmer if...
your tractor cost more than your house.
                                    -Amos Metzler

There are all kinds of farms in this world. Crop farms. Pig farms. Horse farms. Goat farms. Sheep farms. Well, you get the idea.

Then there are dairy farms.

They are set apart, not because they have cattle- even ranches have those- but because the farmers who run dairy farms are a type of hybrid society. It's like they took regular-ole farmer and bred in a good solid dose of crazy.

13

Don't misunderstand. Crazy is not a synonym for unintelligent. Farmers, in general, are more intelligent than most of the world's population.

You don't believe me? Just take a few of those high-falooting, degree-toting university folks, throw them on a farm and say, "Here, feed yourselves, and while you're at it? Provide food for the rest of society as well."

Mmhmm. We'd all be dead within a year.

But dairy farmers really are crazier than most all the rest.

Think about it. There are plenty of animals that give milk. Goats. Sheep. Relatively small and intelligent creatures. But what do dairy farmers milk? Fifteen hundred pounds of stupid.

Hence, by the fifth time a wet sloppy tail loaded with manure hits you, a little bit of crazy just leaks right in. It's a simple hazard of the job.

There are positive elements to dairy farming as well.

There is fresh milk from the tank, which makes the store-bought stuff taste like watered down sewage. Food that comes to your table from the barn or the fields instead of the grocery store. Cattle grazing out in your fields and the ability to work together with your family, which is priceless.

There are, of course, flies on dairy farms but think of all the millions of people who live in cities where there is smog, which is just as annoying and doesn't die in the winter.

Still, the hazards abound.

We had a fresh heifer one year that I affectionately called "the dancing heifer." She did an impressive two-step whenever I walked into the stall with her, the milking unit dangling from my hands.

Her eyes would widen, her hips would swing, and I would start sweet-talking.

Any good dairy farmer can sweet talk, even the rough and tough trash-talking ones. Especially if it's a high-bred heifer you're trying to work with. Chances are she's worth a good chunk of change and you're expecting her to crank out enough milk to earn her keep, so it's either sweet talk or lose your temper—and screaming just makes 'em jump higher.

For the first several milkings a new heifer will be "milked out" so the colostrum can be saved for the calf and all the antibodies in it won't raise the somatic cell count in the clean milk. On our farm we use an old fashioned milking can for this, so the unsellable milk doesn't go through the pipeline.

On this particular morning I was sweet-talking away and she was doing her little dance-routine as I hooked up the milking can. Suddenly a stray hoof caught the hose.

I jumped back until I was practically underneath the neighboring cow as the hose went one direction and the milk pail another. The vacuum line was yanked off so forcefully the cap went flying as well, causing great noise and even greater confusion.

By the time I was done muttering about how good fresh hamburgers are, the heifer settled down and stood there, sweet-as-you-please, looking over her shoulder at me. I followed her gaze and saw the milk pail, lid tossed off, beautiful white milk turning a dark chocolate brown as it sat in the full gutter, manure dripping down the sides.

I'm sure the sight that followed was humorous, at least to her. For the only thing to do when a heifer goes crazy and tosses the milking pail into the gutter is to go after it. And unless you keep rubber gloves in your back pocket, you'll be forced to give yourself a beauty-routine known as the "manure mask."

The real problem with manure is that the smell doesn't really wash off. It wears off. Over a course of several days and a dozen showers.

As I stood in line at the grocery store later that day, it was quite easy to read the expression of the lady behind me. "Good grief," her look said, "couldn't this girl shower before coming out in public?"

I did, sweet lady, I did. And if you dislike the smell that much, I suggest moving to a county where there are more people than cattle. You're a bit outnumbered here.

LIVING IN DAIRY FARMER COUNTRY

You might be a Dairy Farmer if...

all the church events are scheduled around milking time.

- Delite Lago

Dairy farmers are funny creatures. They're quite talkative most of the time, but there are a few instances where they can be as tight-lipped as a sealed canning jar.

Take for instance, if you have an issue with one of your cows. You can pull a seasoned farmer aside, show them the problem and say, "So, what do you think?" and they'll grunt, nod, look carefully at the issue and mutter a variation of "It's hard to know..."

So you'll call the vet, they'll come out and tell you some scientific mumbo-jumbo, charge you $400 and the cow will die three days later.

You'll stumble through, trying this and that. You'll bury another cow or two, take a bad dip on milk, and when you finally get to say, "I figured out…" and fork up your gleaned information, those blasted seasoned farmers will either affirm or deny it with a bit of a smirk.

But most of the time it's a kind smirk. And the ones who know you best might wink and add, "I knew you'd figure it out."

Over time you'll realize that you have to wait for the offered tips and tuck them away. Step back, give 'em enough time, and the information is bound to leak out.

The off-handed comment, like, "Get colostrum into a new calf and the mortality rate will jump at least 90%," or, "If you have any extra colostrum, you might want to freeze it because not every cow gives some," will roll of their tongues at the strangest moments. Then all these weird little tips will pile up and suddenly you'll find yourself diagnosing milk fever, breech calves, pregnancy, cysts, sore knees, split hips and parasites.

But under no circumstances should you ask a direct question. Just shut up and listen.

YOU MIGHT BE A DAIRY FARMER IF...
you can't remember the names of your relatives
but you remember the names and milking stats
of each and every cow.

- Karen Lehman

Some lessons on the farm come hard and quick. You don't have to wait for another farmer to share them because you learn 'em on the first day. Like *don't face the back of a cow while cleaning their udder.* Two words. Tail. Manure.

The next lesson comes right on the heels of the first. You can complain, opening your mouth and receiving a nice taste of manure, or you can just wipe off the crap and keep working.

The world could be a better place if more people would learn that lesson, eh?

YOU MIGHT BE A DAIRY FARMER IF...
the term "I grabbed her teat"
doesn't seem offensive.

- Sarah Lehman

Dairy farmers have a few idiosyncrasies that are hard to swallow. Number one being that they compare women to heifers. As wrong as it sounds, if a dairy farmer says, "You're a pretty little heifer," it really is a compliment. They don't just throw that phrase around.

On the other hand, if you're ever compared to a "heifer in heat," you may want to learn to flirt a little more covertly. Those who have worked around a heifer and found her front hooves up on their shoulders will understand this phrase a bit better.

You might be a Dairy Farmer if...
you've had huge bowls of whipped cream and ice cream because the winter storms kept the milk truck away.
- Ken Siegrist

Dairy farmers are an independent lot. They're pretty addicted to being their own boss and heaven help you if you step onto their territory and try to do things your own way. Each farmer has their own system, their own tried-and-true way of making the most milk. Their methods can be as different as the sun to the moon, but they swear by them.

It's a lot of responsibility, being self-employed, so they develop survival skills. Like, for example, getting up at ridiculous hours to go to the barn.

I mean, who in the world ever started getting up at three in the morning to milk the cows? I think it was probably some farmer on a power trip.

"I'm my own boss," he told himself one day and just to prove his point, he went to work in the middle of the night.

And sure enough, it caught on. Farmer after farmer jumped at the chance to be finishing up barn work while the lowly employed people were just beginning their jobs.

Of course, it back-fired on them because when the employed people head home at five, farmers are dragging their feet back out to the barn.

Dairy farming is still attractive to men despite all the hard work. It all comes back to the independence. You make the product, sell the product and have a certain level of control. Oh, the government tries to pretend that they control things. They send out crazy regulations, created by people who have never set foot on a farm, nor have any understanding of cattle, but it's okay. They can only push so far before the dairy farmers get cranky.

The big farms, they take to spreading the milk as fertilizer on their fields and the little farms, they whip up a nice big batch of cheese.

It may not change the world, or the government, but it sure feels good to stick your tongue out at the bullies once in awhile.

YOU MIGHT BE A DAIRY FARMER IF...

you see most sunrises through
the barn windows.

- Julie Roggie

Field work is what redeems farming. The breeze, the earth, the smell of the sun and the rain. Farmers thrive on it.

Except when disaster happens. It is then that stress comes so rapidly, they develop ulcers in a matter of minutes. This, perhaps, excuses their propensity for craziness.

You think I'm kidding, don't you?

Around the year 2002, my then-single husband bought a discbine. It was shiny. A red New Idea 5209. He was in the custom business and was looking forward to a year with less breakdowns and more productivity. It was a great plan.

On the second field of the season, after being assured by the land owner that the field was clear, he ran that shiny machine right over a baby grand piano.

Now you really think I'm kidding, don't you?

True story. The remains of an ancient baby grand piano, with the legs and wood torn off leaving a 250 pound cast iron shell with hay growing out of it, was mulched through the teeth of a machine with less than one season of hay through it. A cloud of smoke and then dead silence. How do you even explain that to someone?

Those of you who aren't farmers are probably snickering and the rest of you are moaning along with my husband. He doesn't even like to hear the story, it still leaves him with a sick feeling in his stomach.

I asked him one time if the piano played any music when it went through the mower. "Yeah," he said, "the kind that goes *cha-ching, cha-ching, cha-ching.*"

He told the owner of the field about the situation and the man nodded and rubbed his face, "Oooh, that's right," he said, "I was hauling that thing to the junk and it fell off my wagon. Forgot about it. Thanks for finding it for me."

Right. You're welcome.

YOU MIGHT BE A DAIRY FARMER IF...

you keep a jar of Ovaltine in the milkhouse.

- Ken Siegrist

Every farmer has their favorite tractor manufacturer. There are Case International men, John Deere men, Allis Chalmers men, Ford men, Deutz men, New Holland men… the list goes on.

John Deere, of course, holds the most followers. They have done a stunning job at marketing. It's quite impressive.

My father-in-law, as a tractor mechanic, often gets asked what type of tractor is the best. He'll hem and haw around for a while, telling you the strengths and weakness of half a dozen models before someone asks the loaded question, "What do you think of John Deere tractors?"

The question is loaded because John Deere fans are almost always *die-hard* fans. They have John Deere tractors and toys and calendars and Christmas cards and hats and sweatshirts. They paint things green and buy Johnny Tractor storybooks for their children.

They ask the question but it's a bit like they're wearing a big green sign warning you to watch your step.

My father-in-law, he just gets a bit of a twinkle in his eye before responding and saying, truthful as the day is long, "I appreciate John Deere. They have fed my family for many years."

YOU MIGHT BE A DAIRY FARMER IF...

you wake up to the sound of a car horn and immediately think: "The cows are out!"

- Ken Siegrist

Most of the world has a twisted view of dairy farmers. They think farmers are people who couldn't swing college. The not-so-smart or not-so-classy who shovel manure because that's all they can do.

Just the idea proves the ignorance of those who believe it.

Farmers are actually some of the smartest in all of society. Not just in common sense, though they definitely rank high in that area, but in dozens of other areas as well.

You don't believe me?

Go ahead, tell me: how many square feet to the acre? Okay, now tell me how many acres will a bag of 80,000 corn seeds plant?

What day should you plant the 82 day corn and what day should you plant the 106 day corn? What percent moisture should the corn be before you chop? How many degrees does the soil need to be before you can put the early corn in the ground?

Oh, don't worry, the questions are just beginning. There are dozens, for every variety of plants, every slight change in the weather.

It's a bit like one of those story-problems from math class… on steroids.

You have two cobs of corn. One from 106 day corn planted on May 6th. The other from 82 day corn planted on June 9th. The 106 day corn is 37% moisture on October 21st. The 82 day corn is at 38.6% moisture on the same day.

The cobs are almost identical in size and the 82 day corn was planted after a cutting of hay was taken off the field. The hay yielded 890 bales sold for $2.75 a bale.

The 82 day corn was planted on plowed sod, top dressed with $500 worth of nitrogen. The 106 day corn was planted on old corn ground with regular fertilizer.

Which corn will be the most profitable?

Oh, and do not forget to take into account the GDD (Growing Degree Days) which can be calculated by using this formula:

GDD = (T High plus T Low) divided by 2, minus 50

Mmhmm... that's what I thought. Slow, my friends? Farmers are not slow. Or anywhere behind all the college-educated folks in the world. They are miles ahead.

Besides mathematics, they know *biology* (crop rotations, soil balance), *meteorology* (weather patterns), *animal husbandry* (cultivation, management and production of domestic animals, including improvement of the qualities desired), *veterinary medicine* (diagnosing and treating ill or injured animals), *mechanics* (fixing or replacing any number of machines in the course of the day, including but not limited to: vacuum pumps, silo un-loaders, small engines, elevators, etc...), *nutritional science* (feeding and care of animals), as well as having skills in carpentry, large machinery operation, and electrical science.

And the best part? Farmers work out these math problems just for fun. They sit around with a couple cobs of corn and discuss every variation, weather pattern, and soil type that could possibly alter the crop ratio. It's what they do to relax.

A bit different than watching something on Neflix, eh?

Yes, dairy farmers are funny creatures. But they're *smart* funny creatures and the world would do better to listen a bit closer to their wisdom.

YOU MIGHT BE A DAIRY FARMER IF...

when a guy is bragging up his six-pack you think, "Pal, you wouldn't last a thousand square bales."

Farming is Hard
(and I'm thankful for it)

Last January we had a heifer freshen in. She wasn't named previously but quickly earned the handle *Kangaroo*. The moment you moved toward her stall she would jump a foot into the air.

In the midst of one of those jumps, she moved sideways and landed on my right foot. The bruise wrapped from one side to the other and from my ankle to my toes. But I could still walk. Thankfully.

I limped for a week and then the pain settled to a dull ache. In hindsight, I probably should have gotten an x-ray. I'm fairly certain I must have broken or fractured a few bones. This is an assumption based on the fact that over two years later, it still bothers me. I can ignore it most of the time but it's particularly bad right before a storm.

Farming is rough. It can beat you right up and leave you wondering what in the world possessed you to attempt such a thing. It can wear away at your body and strength until all you can think about is *just one day off.*

I love the beauty and the dirt and the harshness and the peace. I love the rush of getting crops in and the warm summer days watching them grow. I love running barefoot through the grass and digging in rich soil. I love the animals and the sound of cows chewing their cud and the scent of hay as bales are broken open and fed. I love that I work with my husband and whatever kids that happen to be around can be included and taught about life and work and food and environment.

But it is hard.

It's hard to be caught tight on a schedule and not be able to enjoy evenings with friends (very often, anyway). It's hard to struggle through the months when my husband's back is hurting and I'm left to milk alone. It's hard when the barn takes all of my energy and the house gets messier and messier and suddenly, someone stops in and frowns at the pile of dirty dishes and the dirt on the floor. It's hard when some friendships fall away because, to be honest, *it's impossible to understand the demands of farming unless you farm.* It's exceptionally hard when there is unexplained stray voltage in your barn killing off an entire crop of new calves, leaving you with no replacements and milk prices dropping.

It's hard when you're left to deal with dead animals and all the gruesomeness of birth and sickness and diseases.

Yet, I'm thankful. *Oh, so very thankful.*

I'm thankful for the land. The way our farm spreads out in every direction and the way the sun rises and sets over it. I'm thankful for the way that God speaks to me through the beauty and the glory.

I'm thankful for the hard work. For the knowledge of hard days of labor that last from morning to night and understanding that *this is what it takes to sustain life.*

Even if you buy your food from a store, *someone, somewhere,* worked to provide it.

I'm thankful for real food. For the ability to bring milk from my cows into my kitchen and turn it into butter and cheese and yogurt. For the vegetables that grow in my garden, the wheat in my fields. For the beef and the pork that come to my freezer from my barn. For the eggs with rich dark yolks that are bursting with vitamins and health-benefits aplenty.

I'm thankful that I've learned dependence on my true strength.

There was a time, a few months back, when my husband had to leave town for several days. The second day of feeding hay had left my hands raw and blistered. We have wire-tied bales and I couldn't find the wire cutters. (My husband has since bought me a pretty pink pair that are *all mine.*) But that evening I stood in the manger and cried because my hands hurt so badly and *I had no choice but to keep hurting them.*

And God spoke, right there in the manger (why would that surprise me?) and said, *Why don't you ask me for strength?* So I did.

I finished feeding the hay without a single blister breaking open. The next morning my brother stopped in to see how I was doing. He tore apart the bales with his callused, work-worn hands and I wept in awe of a God who is faithful.

There are so many ways that farming has blessed my life. So many ways that I've learned and partaken in God's grace for me through this dependence on soil and rain and inner strength.

And today, *again,* I am thankful for this hard thing in my life. *I'm thankful for farming.*

The Thing about Dairy Farmers' Wives

You might be a dairy farmer's wife if...
you know the term "freshened"
isn't referring to powdering your nose.

Dairy farmers' wives are a piece of work. I know. Personally.

They fall into two categories:

- The ones that love the lifestyle of farming.
- The ones who hate every. single. manure. covered. item.

But love it or hate it, wives are predictable.

They all have one thing on the farm they will never do. For some, it's milking. For others, tank washing or calf feeding. Some don't fix gutter cleaners, or do tractor driving, or hay-baling.

For me? I don't spread manure. Ever.

I'll ride along but I won't drive the tractor and spreader. The number one reason? I don't know how. (I may or may not have closed my eyes when my husband tried to show me which levers to push.)

You might be a ~~Dairy Farmer~~ Dairy Farmer's WIFE if...
going on a family picnic means packing up
the food and children and meeting
your husband in whatever field he is working in.

- Julie Roggie

We all have another thing in common. There are always, *always* things to do.

Friends will say, "Let's go here," or "Let's do this," and it's not that we *can't,* it's simply that we have to decide if a night out with girlfriends is worth all the extra work piled up at home.

As one farmer's wife said, "I walk back into the house and it's like I'm being punished for ever daring to leave. There is manure tracked across the floor, extra thick in front of the refrigerator, dishes piled a mile high (after only one night!), and laundry spilling out of the dryer where someone obviously went looking for a particular item of clothing but couldn't be bothered to remove the entire load. I suppose it's not personal but it sure feels like it."

She's right. It's not personal. It's just a bit like a fairy tale. In the books, the princess will turn into a pumpkin if she's gone too long (or something like that), and in real life, if you're gone too long the entire family will turn into pigs.

YOU MIGHT BE A ~~DAIRY FARMER~~ Dairy Farmer's WIFE IF...
"going out" with your husband
means attending a co-op dinner
or dealership open house.
- Julie Roggie

Dairy wives are either the most high-strung women you've ever met or the most laid back.

I went for laid back. Leave your boots on, the floor is dirty anyway. What? You need some coffee? Let me wash a cup.

The high-strung ones can fall into a panic when you come in the wrong door with your barn boots on. "Wait!" they'll scream, "I don't want my kitchen to smell like manure!" and, if it's a bad day, they may just burst into tears.

It can be a constant battle to keep the house presentable, so at a certain point, it might be best to change your idea of presentable. Farming is the bitter enemy of a clean house and there *are* worse things than muddy floors. Like, for example, hungry men arriving when you don't have any food ready.

History books always make it sound so great. It used to be that harvest time came and all the families would travel from farm to farm. The women would make food and set up tables while the men worked... those were the days.

Now the men travel from farm to farm without their wives. Come lunch time, the majority of these men end up at my house. So I've learned to master the ten-minute meals.

Never heard of those?

Meat thaws in five to seven minutes in a sink full of hot water. Spaghetti cooks in eight. Meat fries in two. Vegetables cook in four. Sauce heats in one or less. Whalla.

Usually I finish, plop it all on the table, sit down, and someone will say, "Uhm, do we get silverware with this?"

Good grief. Some people just aren't grateful enough.

YOU MIGHT BE A ~~DAIRY FARMER~~ IF...

Dairy Farmer's WIFE

when the milk turns sour you just
change the breakfast menu
to pancakes.

- Anne Siegrist

Farmers speak another language. Any dairyman's wife will tell you the same thing. Oh, it sounds like English but it's really not. It's Farmer.

For example, your husband comes into the house with a smile and a sweet peck on the cheek. After a minute of chit-chat he'll say, "Honey, let's go for a little drive." Sounds like a simple English sentence, doesn't it? Don't be fooled. The actual meaning of this phrase is *Let's drive around until we see another farmer out, then we'll stop and chat for a couple hours.* That project you were going to accomplish this afternoon? Just resign yourself now.

Another similar phrase is, "Come with me to pick up some parts?" This is a tricky one. If you ask questions he'll insist that he is running in to grab the parts and then right back out. He just wants you to ride along because he loves you and wants to spend time with you. Be forewarned. When he says, "It'll just be a few minutes," the translation is actually, *Bring a book. Maybe two.*

When I first married my farmer, no one warned me that he would be continually spouting off strange combinations of numbers and expect me to know what he was referring to. 4210, 2470, 3950, 930. My brain kept trying to calculate random algebra problems. *x- 4210/2470 = u r crazy.*

Thankfully, I eventually learned the simple translation. *A tractor.* That's it. That's all. No need to figure out anything else. He's just talking about a tractor. *Whew.*

You might be a ~~Dairy Farmer~~ *Dairy Farmer's WIFE* if...

you get all kinds of excited
over polka-dotted barn boots.

Understanding Farmer is essential to a happy marriage. There are so many things that can get lost in the translation. Take for example this simple statement, "Dinner will be ready in fifteen minutes? Okay, let me finish this one thing." Any normal English speaking person would assume this to mean he will be back in about fifteen minutes. It actually does not. He's really saying *I'll be back in an hour or two.*

See the difficulty here?

During spring and throughout summer you'll probably hear this romantic phrase, "Can I take you for a four-wheeler ride?" Aww, you think as you snuggle in behind him, leaning your head against his muscled shoulder, and smiling about how glad you are that your husband is still crazy for you. He probably is, but don't let this sentence throw you for a loop. What he actually means is, *Let's go look at the corn. Maybe it grew since we checked it this morning.*

Another phrase that no one ever warned me about is, again, seemingly innocent. You'll be busy doing your own work and he'll stick his head in the door, a five o'clock shadow darkening his face, the faint scent of cow manure clinging to him, and say, "Uhm, Hon?" Dear ones, this is a killer phrase. Brace yourself. It actually means: *I need you to do something horrendously scary like drive a enormous tractor beside a huge drop-off* or pull another tractor out of ten feet of mud *OR* (my personal favorite) *help me set up the bulldozer that accidently tipped over while I was driving it.*

The best, of course, are the days when you're happily working in the kitchen cooking a meal for your sweet little family and he comes barging into the house. "Think you can add a couple plates to the table?" he'll ask, an urgent look around his eyes. The actual meaning of the sentence is simple: *I hope you have a lot of extra quick food ready because there are, like, fifteen hungry guys out here and I just invited them all in for lunch.*

And once again you're back to the ten minute meals. This time you might try chili. Not the from-scratch, win-the-chili-cook-off type, but rather the from-cans-and-meatless type. You know, the one where you open five cans of beans, four jars of tomatoes, a jar of salsa and throw a few handfuls of chili powder into a pot and bring it to a boil. If you're lucky you might still have bread in the house and can even add in some garlic toast to top off the whole shebang.

The men, they'll think you're amazing. Compliments will fill your kitchen as they wolf down the food and you'll be left to daydream about the amazing chili you once made with so much color and flavor that it seemed to dance in your mouth. The kind that takes a full day to cook so the flavors can nestle in together and fill the house with the hearty smell of warmth and spice. *Those were the days*, you'll sigh as you clear the table and brush the crumbs onto the floor.

You'll clean them up later, after milking, if you have energy then.

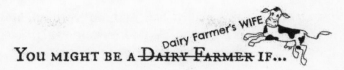

You might be a ~~Dairy Farmer~~ Dairy Farmer's WIFE if...

your garden plot is larger
than your yard.

- Ken Siegrist

Once you learn the language, it's really not so bad. The surprises are limited (farmers are predictable after all) and unromantic-romantic gestures are still worth something in the end. You just close your eyes and snuggle your head against his shoulder and pretend that the only reason he cares about the corn is because it's a chance to sneak away with you for a few minutes. And just watch, if you can muster up a bit of excitement and exclaim over the little shoots of green, he'll probably reward you with a bear hug and a tender kiss. And for just a moment, the world will be a perfect place.

You might be a ~~Dairy Farmer~~ Dairy Farmer's WIFE if...

you've ever worn a winter hat
to the barn in the middle of summer
to keep your hair clean.

Farmers can be so rushed, so hard working, and so exasperating it can be easy to miss the sacrifices they make for their wives.

When my father-in-law was a young man, he worked from sun up until sun down and he often requested that his wife work with him. She would drive tractor or work in the fields beside him for hours a day.

Now, if you don't pay close attention when listening to their stories, it would seem that he wasn't very romantic.

Yet, the truth is that he knew, deep down, how desperately he needed her and his romantic actions were there, they were just more practical than pretty.

Like the day she was driving an old Allis Chalmers WD with a rebuilt engine and a heavy load behind it. She started down a steep hill and when she applied the breaks, the tractor went into a skid, the load pushing her down the road.

Her husband, seeing her in danger, ran to her and raced beside the tractor, giving her instructions on how to steer. He never left her, running all the way down the hill, and was ready to help her bail off or throw himself into harm's way to keep her safe.

And in true farmer-fashion, after he got his wife to safety, he went out and bought a brand-new tractor, fresh off the lot.

He was a mechanic. If it was just him, he would have used rebuilt machinery all his life. But for his wife? He'd make sure there was always the best for her to drive so she would never be in that situation again.

In our fairy-tale imaginations we often think romance is sweet words or bouquets of flowers or grand gestures. At least, that's how the movies portray it. But I suggest that true romance is the husband who will run right beside you when you're in danger, the one who will never leave your side. The one who will work even harder to give you the things that he would never buy for himself.

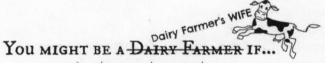

You might be a ~~**Dairy Farmer**~~ Dairy Farmer's WIFE **if...**
you've learned not to hang out
the laundry when your husband
is spreading manure.

- Jennifer Metzler

My husband is a mechanic as well, like his father before him. We have any number of tractors on the farm at any given time. But always, always, he keeps a tractor with easy controls and a nice seat for me to run even though there are many days that you'll see him standing on an old relic, the seat broken beneath him. *That's romance.*

And it's not just me. I hear the men talking. They buy the new balers so their wives can work with them without having to climb in and out of the tractor a dozen times to fix little problems. They buy the new, lighter milking units. They remodel barns. They deal with ornery heifers who don't milk worth a hoot, just because their wives have a soft-spot for the blasted thing.

They do the things they would never do for themselves, spend money, build and sweat and work—just because they love.

So we must look careful and listen intently and slowly, softly, we'll see the truth. That these smart, hard-working, ornery farmers are actually the romantic, deep-loving type. And we are reminded, just in case we forgot with all the manure soaked clothing and long hours of work that distract us, we married the very best of the best.

You MIGHT BE A ~~DAIRY FARMER~~ Dairy Farmer's WIFE IF...
your wedding had to be at noon,
so all the other farmers wouldn't have
to miss a milking to attend.

Found Gold

My hands were covered in blood and manure.

The new little calf fought my offer of milk from the bottle. She swung her head and tugged at her rope. The mother hadn't licked off the baby and the remains of birth, manure, and hay covered the shivering body. I knew the warm colostrum that I was trying to force down its throat would make the difference between living and dying.

I moved my left hand to pry open its mouth and my diamond winked at me from amidst the filth.

A lot of women take off their rings to do dirty work. I did for the first few months of my marriage.

There was a spot on the windowsill that I would drop the shiny diamond and leave it safe until my hands were clean once again.

One day I went to get it and couldn't find it. My heart skipped two beats. I started pulling things apart when I heard a chuckle behind me. I spun around and my mischievous husband's gaze met mine. He dropped to one knee and proposed again.

"Why did you have it off?" he asked after I had once again accepted and the ring was back where it belonged.

"I was kneading bread dough." I pointed to the loaves now rising on the back of the woodstove.

"No need for that." He kissed my cheek. "I bought it for you so it could be worn. Not protected."

After that day, the only time it left my finger was while I was standing in Zales, waiting for it to be cleaned. The moment it was handed back, I put it on again.

This morning in the barn, I was struck by how out of place it looked. Smears of filth and a diamond that catches light and makes rainbows.

My ring is white gold. There are different types, but mine is a yellow gold band dipped in a mixture that contains other metals to lighten the color. I loved it when it was new. It shimmered.

But life has been rough on it. Years of filth and cleanings have left it dull. The last time I stopped for a cleaning the lady informed me, "You'll want to send it to get dipped soon. The white gold coating is getting thin." She picked up the ring and pointed. "See, right here. The real gold is showing through."

I told my husband when I got home. He started smiling. "Good."

"Good?" I questioned.

"Sure." He pulled me into a hug. "It's a lot more valuable to have a ring that shows wear than to have a shiny new one. Anyone can get a new one. Very few have theirs long enough for it to be worn."

He had a point.

Then he laughed. "Besides, it's the real gold that is showing through. That's the valuable stuff."

And the valuable stuff is what can stand up to the pressures of life. The dirt and filth. The cleanings. The bread dough. The manure. The bloody mess.

Everything else of lesser value just fades away. And what's left is real.

Oh, God. Make me more concerned with what's real than with what shimmers.

The Thing About Dairy Cows

You might be a dairy farmer if...
sandpaper makes you think
of a cow's tongue.

I am thoroughly convinced that the best spelling of the word cow is S-T-U-P-I-D. I'm not being mean, I'm just being honest. Dairy cattle are as dumb as a box of rocks.

We've bred the survival instinct right out of them. Don't believe me? Go ahead and pick up a registered heifer and put her in a stall beside a half-breed. Throw some hay in front of them and watch.

The registered heifer will eat whatever is directly in front of her and then beller and beller, or worse, drop onto her knees and give herself a swollen knee and limp around for days. And if you paid a lot of money for her? She'll probably die.

The half-breed, she'll look at the idiot next to her, stretch out her neck and eat all the hay in a ten foot radius.

Later, the registered heifer (if she survived) will freshen in and give you 80-100 pounds of milk a day, which is good because she'll need stall mats and constant attention and astronomical vet bills.

The half-breed will shell out 30-65 pounds of a milk a day and all you'll have to do is feed and water her. Talk about simplicity.

Still, it's a lot more fun to be able to say, "Yep, yep, those cows of mine are really pumping out the milk. Yous guys should see 'em."

And those registered ones? They look pretty at the fair. All combed and washed and bedded up with thirty dollars worth of straw.

Just try and make sure the hay stays up close to their noses.

YOU MIGHT BE A DAIRY FARMER IF...
you know that the term "free martin"
isn't slang for a free martini.

It's a good thing dairy farmers are a bit on the crazy side, otherwise there'd be a severe shortage of milk in the world.

Think about it.

Beef cattle are penned up and fed until they're nice and fat. The interaction between the cow and rancher is little at most, and they end with the animal dead.

Dairy cattle? We spend hours a day sitting under their back feet.

Are you catching what I'm saying here?

Dairy farmers get stepped on, splattered, squashed, and licked.

Our goal is not a fat, dead animal, it's a live, milking one. Turns out that when you want an animal alive, they like to try and die. When you get in the way of that, they like to run you over. In fact, once in awhile you'll find an animal that just plain wants *you* dead.

Take for example, the heifer my grandpa had back in the sixties. She was stubborn as a mule and meaner than a hornet.

One day while they were bringing the cows in from the field, she got the idea in her sassy big head that Grandpa would be better off pinned against the wall, rather than directing traffic.

She charged once, head down and hoofs flying. He sidestepped and said (sweetly, I'm sure), "Cut it out!" She turned and with a wild look in her eye, came right back at him.

So, he did the only thing any sane farmer would do. He clanked her in the head with the handle of his pitchfork.

Later he would say, a bit flabbergasted, "I was just trying to remind her who was in charge. Guess I reminded her a bit too hard."

She fell right down then shook her head a few times before standing back up. She never was quite right after that. Acted half dopey most of the time. Which, by the way, is preferable to acting like a murdering, bull-headed brute.

YOU MIGHT BE A DAIRY FARMER IF...
you ever drank milk in a well-aimed
stream straight from the cow.

- Ken Siegrist

Cattle eat metal. You know, bolts, screws, and pieces of wire.

Turns out that kills them eventually. Even with four stomachs, they can't digest stainless steel.

The only hope for a cow with hardware is a magnet. Can you imagine someone coming up to you and trying to force feed you a magnet? Exactly. Now try to imagine grabbing hold of a cow's head, which is connected to a couple thousand pounds of flesh, and forcing one down its throat. Are you beginning to understand why farmers started dehorning their animals?

YOU MIGHT BE A DAIRY FARMER IF...
there is something comforting
in the smell of a warm barn
and the sound of softly chewing cud.

- Katie Bernier

My mom grew up on a farm but she was the youngest and the only girl with six older brothers. Yes, she was spoiled. No, she didn't do much for barn chores.

One day she decided to go brush her horse down. As she was walking through the barn, she noticed a couple of cows that looked raggedy. They hadn't been clipped in awhile and their hair was all tangled.

She had the curry comb right in her hand, so she stepped up between them and started brushing. It felt good to be helping with the chores and the cow seemed to like it just fine.

After a bit she turned and started in on the next one. It wasn't long until she noticed that it was getting a bit hard to breathe. She pushed her hip into the leaning cow and told her to move over.

Turns out cows don't listen to voice commands quite as well as horses do.

The two cows had their hips pressed tight together and Mom was left with two options. She could go up through the stanchions, an option that she quickly ruled out because back then they *didn't* dehorn the cattle. Or she had to go over the back of the cow.

Elbows pressed into the first fifteen hundred pound animal, hip pressed hard into the second fifteen hundred pound animal, she made a flying scrambling leap.

Turns out that was the last time she willingly helped with the cows.

Any good dairy man will tell you that getting caught between two cows who are refusing to move apart is a simple hazard of the job.

You quickly learn the techniques required for body-slamming three quarters of a ton of solid animal flesh.

But there are the horror stories. Arms getting pinned down. Wind getting knocked out. Feet getting stepped on. Heifers going wild.

I've never heard of anyone dying from this but that is little comfort when you can't breathe, even to call for help.

It was my husband who told me that the way to direct a cow is to turn her nose. The first time a couple animals decided to pin me in the stall, I reached into my memory and grabbed the closest bit of information that I could find. Cows follow the direction of their noses.

Without further ado, I reached forward and grabbed a hunk of hair underneath the offending animal's chin and turned her to face me. In my best mother-voice I lit into her like a haystack afire.

After giving her a good tongue lashing, I pushed her nose away from me. Sure enough, her body followed.

I was astounded at the usefulness of this particular technique. I began using it for everything. A cow kicks off its milker? Grab her nose and lecture her. A cow won't stand still? Lecture her. A cow won't go in the right stall? Lecture her. A cow looks at you funny? Lecture her.

It wasn't until almost a year later that I found out most dairy farmers don't jerk their cow's heads around and lecture them with a finger pointed at their nose.

My father-in-law was visiting on the morning of this particular acquisition of knowledge. Amos left to work with him and I was finishing up milking alone. Or so I thought.

It was a lovely morning, the sun shining in the barn windows, the sweet smell of baleage in the air. I was singing a lively hymn and was happily planning my day when Old Red decided that she didn't want to wear her milker.

My voice was echoing through the barn, "I'll fly away, O glory, I'll fly a… I don't know what you're thinking, you ridiculous animal, but when I put the milker on, you had better leave it there! Oh, don't you kick at me, come here. You. Come here. Get your face over here. Now listen and you listen good. *Do not kick your milker off.* Do you understand me? ...O glory, I'll fly away. When I die, hallelujah by and by, I'll fly away."

A few minutes later my husband came downstairs to share the humor with me. Apparently you can hear quite well in the hay mow.

They had been working away, listening to me sing, and my poor father-in-law froze when my voice dropped into lecture mode, unsure of what to do. When I started singing again he said quietly, "I thought for a minute she was in serious trouble."

My husband just smirked, "I'd say it was the cow that was in trouble, Pa."

You might be a Dairy Farmer if...
women sharing their birth stories
cause you to bite your tongue
to keep from comparing their experiences
to the cow that just freshened in.

Of all the terms used in the dairy farming world, *freshening* is the most ridiculous. They take a perfect normal, used-fairly-regularly word and make it mean, "coming into milk production" (a.k.a. giving birth). The first time a farmer said that he had to hurry home because a heifer was freshening

57

in, I looked at him a bit cross-eyed. *Does he know the actual meaning of that word?* I wondered.

Of course, the only time I heard the phrase was when I was watching movies from the Regency era and an elderly matron would inform the gentlemen that the ladies were "freshening up" in the side room between dances.

Just so you know, the context can change the meaning of words a great deal.

When we bought our first herd of cows there was a big black and white Holstein in the mix. She was called "Mine," which was a very confusing name to be sure.

One evening we noticed that Mine was getting ready to freshen. We watched her a bit, but were certain it would be quite a while yet, so we opted to head to bed and check on her in the morning.

At first light we meandered out to the barn and found her standing in her stall, happily munching on hay. There was afterbirth in the gutter behind her and she was dripping milk, which were great signs— except we had one small problem. There wasn't a calf.

Of course, there *had* to be a calf. So we searched the barn from end to end. Amos even went out through the gutter shoot, just in case the little creature had decided to go for a ride in the manure spreader.

We found nothing. Not a trace. I don't mind telling you that we were completely flabbergasted.

"Check the gutters again," Amos told me, as he went to look at the practically-clear mangers once more.

I walked up and down the length of the barn, staring into the crap-filled gutters. All I found was manure, straw and the hay that wasteful cows had thrown back.

We reconvened near the front of the barn, fifteen cows down from where Mine stood, perfectly content to eat her hay and not worry about her vanishing offspring.

"I'm not sure what to do," Amos said. He looked down right then and reached over to grab my arm. With the other hand he pointed toward the gutter by our feet.

There was an eyeball, blinking owlishly at us.

Unbeknownst to us, the big black and white Holstein had been bred to a Jersey and the teeny-tiny half-breed calf was exactly the color of manure. She fit right down in the gutter, was generously covered with straw and had apparently been sleeping until that moment, when she decided to blink open her eyes, allowing the movement to catch our attention.

She was happily content, soaking in the warm manure and was a bit irritated when we moved her to the cold cement beside her mother. Mine just glanced at her and returned to eating after giving me a look that clearly stated that she had no interest in licking off a manure-soaked runt.

To be honest, I couldn't really blame her.

YOU MIGHT BE A DAIRY FARMER IF...
you've ever been angry enough to spit nails because four cows have stuffed themselves into two stalls.

I never thought of myself as having much of a temper. Until we bought dairy cows, that is. Within the first week I learned a startling truth: cattle who don't go where I want them to cause me to lose my cool quicker than snow on a wood stove.

In fact, tying cows was a good exercise for conflict resolution within my marriage. A few rounds of, "Why were you standing there?" and, "Move, move, move!" and there were some full-blown something-has-to-change-because-I-might-use-this-pitchfork-on-you sessions between my husband and I in the middle of the barn with wandering bovines and cow piles galore.

One time we were both standing there, steam rolling out of our ears, when the hilarity of the situation hit us. "I'm not really mad at you," I finally said around giggles. "It's these ridiculous animals!"

Turns out the best conflict resolution is three deep breaths and a nice belly laugh.

Over time we learned a great lesson. Never be in a hurry while tying cows. They will sense it and spread the word that it's time to play a fun game called, "Let's see how many of us can fit into one stall." It's actually a really crappy game, just so you know, and it's very important not to allow the suggestion to spread very far. Just imagine twelve people stuffed inside a Volkswagen Beetle. Even worse, picture trying to get them out.

If you're not sure how to stop it, I propose giving the instigator a good long lecture. Don't forget to wag your finger at her nose a few times, just for effect.

The Thing About Manure

You might be a dairy farmer if...
manure is a regular topic at
the dinner table.
- *Andrea Steria*

People who don't work on farms have extremely sensitive nostrils. They can sniff out cow manure a mile away. Their little (and sometimes not-so-little) noses wrinkle right up in disgust. "Do you smell that?" they ask, the words drawn out to further indicate the offensiveness of the odor.

In reality, manure is not as disgusting as people make it out to be and is actually a very useful commodity. Rich in nutrients, it is essential for good crop production and any decent farmer will spread it as thick as possible onto his fields.

And gardens. Nothing grows vegetables like manure-soaked dirt.

Back in the seventies, when my grandparents retired from the farm and moved to town, they found themselves in quite a quandary. They still gardened and Grandma greatly missed having access to this quality fertilizer. So, for Mother's Day that year she requested a nice big bucket of manure.

Grandpa happily complied.

For weeks Grandma tried to stretch that manure as far as possible. She spread some onto the garden and then "ripened" more water in the manure pail. The nutrient-rich liquid could then be used on her plants. It worked wonders and she was very pleased with the results.

Except, well, one batch ripened a bit too much. The entire yard smelled so horrendous that even her well-seasoned nose wrinkled in shock. Here they were, living in town like the fancy-folks, and their yard smelled like a dirty diaper had exploded. City people are finicky and there are so many laws and ordnances that she was certain they could be arrested at any moment.

To make matters worse, they found out their neighbor, a lawyer, was having a party the next day. Grandma was just certain he was going to sue them for air pollution.

Because she feared the police showing up and she just plain didn't want anyone to know who had caused the eye-watering scent, she made Grandpa wait until it was dark and then go bury the offending bucket by moonlight.

Only a man who truly loved his wife would dig a hole in the middle of the night to bury a bucket of manure that was so ripe it practically burned your lungs, and Grandpa loved Grandma something fierce.

It still took a bit of time before the scent vanished and she felt safe to wander about outside at will, but eventually the memory of the undercover-crap-concealing-operation faded.

For years she kept the manure burying a secret but she broke down and confessed some time after her eighty-fifth birthday. "I'm pretty sure most all our old neighbors are dead now anyway," she explained. "Not to mention, the air has been polluted by far worse things after this many years." And as far as she knows, the bucket is still buried right where they left it.

You might be a Dairy Farmer if...

the teller at the bank can still smell manure
long after your check is cashed because of
the brown puddle in front of her window.

- Rhonda Freed

Most manure, when not spread on garden plots, is immediately put back onto the fields to boost the quality of the soil. Except when winter settles in. Negative temperatures and spreading manure don't mix very well. When the crap starts to freeze before it hits the ground, you've got a problem. But, as it turns out, the cows don't stop producing manure even when it's cold outside.

Enter the manure pit.

Some farmers have these great big cement contraptions, but we have a regular old hole in the ground. When it's impossible to spread, we pile the manure in the pit and wait for warmer weather.

Unfortunately, the ramp down to our pit opens into one of the hay fields we used to after-feed in the fall. Once the hay has been cut and wrapped in round bales, we let the cows loose to eat what is left until it freezes too hard for grass to grow.

Remember how I mentioned that cows are stupid? Well, periodically they go for a swim.

Just a little tip: Swimming in manure is not actually advised.

It always happens the same way. It will be a dark, rainy night, almost time for evening milking, when my husband will show up at the door with that tired look on his face. "Guess where your cow is?" he asks.

The next thing, I'm driving a tractor with my husband standing in the loader bucket, leaning forward, trying to reach the nitwit who decided on a soak in the crap. Cold rain will be dripping down the back of my neck or the wind will be driving it with enough force to sting my cheeks and she'll come out mooing and stinking to high heaven. Milking that evening is a nightmare.

We normally use reusable wash cloths to clean the cow's udders before milking, but for these precious moments I'll break out the disposable paper towels. Ripe manure that has been sitting in a pit for a period of time is very different than fresh manure. Even farmers can smell that stuff.

It's quite the process to clean the animal up and if it happens on sale days, I'm always tempted to just ship the cow, manure and all.

You might be a Dairy Farmer if...

manure smells like money to you.

- Lonnie Wyse

Besides farmers the only people who seem to be immune to the scent of manure are children.

I watch a three-year-old boy and he is a manure magnet. I can leave him in the middle of a beautifully clean barn floor, all coated in nice white lime, and he will run around happily and somehow, amazingly, find the one single manure pile to fall into. Then he'll stand up, all wide-eyed, and offer me crap-covered hands to clean. I use disposable towels for that job too.

One day he landed flat on his face, arms outstretched, in a huge cow pile. I heard muffled cries and went running to rescue him from an untimely suffocating death. He was covered. Completely and totally covered. There was manure in his ears, up his nose, creased around the corners of his eyes, plastered onto his jacket and pants.

I carried him to the milk house, stripped him bare and turned on the hose. While the water was warming up, I slathered him with soap, working up a nice white lather that quickly turned brown. Once the majority of the caked on stuff had been loosened up, I grabbed the hose and began spraying him off. The poor child had never been hosed down before and took off, screaming at the top of his lungs.

Did you know that it is nigh unto impossible to keep your grip on a soaped up child? They slip right through your fingers like a greased pig.

My husband opened the milk house door in time to see the naked child, head tilted back and screaming like he was being skinned alive, race around the milk tank.

Amos burst into laughter at his hose-wielding wife but quickly muffled it when he saw my face. "Get me the child," I told him, manure-water dripping off my pant legs, "just get me the child."

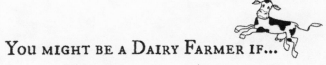

YOU MIGHT BE A DAIRY FARMER IF...

dressing up means having
manure-free clothing on.

Manure is really a necessary evil and over time you stop thinking about it much at all. It's just a part of farming life, the same way that afterbirth, hay bales, cow licks, hard work, flies, and the warm softness of the animals are. They mingle into the painting of life like a sunset that blazes with reds and oranges and purples. Different colors, different aspects, but blended together they can create beauty.

Farmland

by Brianna Siegrist

Why do cows have to smell like a dying diaper,
like a sewage pit,
when the world around is so green and so lovely?
Why do they ruin it with stink piles?
Why, tractors, why the noise?
Why grind gears and let your engine
drown out the song of the Cardinal?
Why, on a sunny afternoon, do the flies circle
endlessly,
the big fat one hitting my cheek,
one crawling on the back of my arm
though I'm trying so hard to ignore them?
Is Eden so impossible?
I ask a few young heifers, contentedly grazing.
They lift their heads and blink their long lashes
and swish their tails and move along.
I ask a green meadow.
It is wide and silent, and sends a dragonfly to buzz

71

like a tiny helicopter,
bringing me the smell of fresh cut alfalfa
from underneath a lazily turning windmill,
but it has no answer for me.
I ask the sun rising over the low distant mountains,
but it is busy dipping the grass in golden dew.
I ask the neighbors, but they wave from the cabs of
their tractors
as they ride out to chop corn
leaving a dozen good brown eggs for my breakfast.
There is no use asking the maples;
in the spring, they will give only their nectar,
in the summer, only their shade.
In the autumn, their shocks of splendor.
There is no use asking the
snowy wonder that blankets the valley in January.
And the song of spring blossoms,
of tulips like bright balloons anchored in every yard
would drown out my words,
If I were still speaking.

Of Life
(and days when everything goes wrong)

I could tell that life was wearing him down. Maybe it was the quiet way he opened the door. Or perhaps the deep slow breaths. Whatever it was that tipped me off, I turned, ready for the look of defeat.

"I don't know how to fix it." The words are clipped and rough. I don't think, in the four years we've been married, that I've ever heard them come out of his mouth. He's been a mechanic for over fifteen years. Fixed hundreds of farm machines. Now, a year into running our own dairy farm, with corn in the fields and snow in the forecast, both choppers are down for the count. One needs money we don't have. The other has a mystery ailment and is sitting in the garage.

I try to think. What can I do? I serve him dinner. Listen to his frustrations. Feel sorry that I have no way of providing him the farm help he so desperately needs. I leave my dishes in the sink and layer on my clothes. I sit in a tractor cab, clicking the switches, waiting, hoping that the chopper arm will turn. It never does.

Finally, when my lips are almost blue and I'm starting to cough, he sends me inside. I walk in feeling the same sense of defeat. My mind scrambles to think of something else. Anything else. I make sure the laundry is switched and his heavy sweatshirts are in the dryer. I pull a hat on, covering my hair, and head out to the barn. He's still working on the chopper when I start milking.

Half way through I am feeling the strain of doing chores myself. But I have to keep working. Doing something. He's trying so hard to run this farm and it seems like I can do so little to ease his burden. I wish I understood mechanics. I wish I could look at the machinery and point out the issue. I wish I could handle the farm work. I wish my back was strong enough. That my wrists, with their tendonitis that flares up after tossing two bales of hay, would be tougher. I wish I could do more.

I'm standing by the little brown jersey when it hits me. In all my attempts to help, all my frustrations with my inability and his need, it never occurred to me.

Oh, God, I stand at my sink every day and pray over the prayer list. My little sister, who is struggling so desperately right now. The woman in my ladies group who is facing a hysterectomy. The friend with a two-month old baby in need of open-heart surgery. And in the middle of all these huge prayer needs, I forget. A day, a week, a month goes by, and I forget that the most important thing I can do for my husband is pray for him.

The last hour of milking, I do the only thing that really matters. I give up on me and the things that come from my strength. I admit my weakness and lean on the One Who is Strong Enough to Form the World with a Word.

And something clicks inside me. *This is it.* The most help I can be. Go to the throne room. Crawl to feet of Jesus. Cry out His name.

I finish milking in silent awe.

Then blinking back tears, I listen as my husband tells the end of the story. The part I couldn't see.

The uncle that showed up to talk. Couldn't help with the chopper but said, "Call me tomorrow, I've got a couple free days. I'll be here. We'll get the corn in."

The phone call from his father. The one that was stuck in Pennsylvania and just made it home. The one who has been a mechanic for much, much longer than fifteen years. More like fifty. "I'll be there tomorrow. We'll get the chopper going," he says.

The next day dawns with hope. They bypass the switch, run a new hose. The chopper arm swings, my husband smiles and waves on his way to the field, I sigh in contentment and joy.

God, help me remember. Only with you, for you, is there purpose and strength. Only in you can I be what my husband needs. And on my knees, I can do the most powerful work of all.

The Untimely Demise of a Kitten Named Butterball

I never liked cats. Not really. They seemed… well, gross. All their licking and hair balls and eating dead rodents.

But then we started milking cows and a half-grown kitten showed up. My husband called her *Gray,* but I dubbed her *KitKat* and "accidently" spilled extra milk while feeding the calves.

She was pretty, stayed at a distance but came running when I called her to get her milk. Kind of like a dog that doesn't lick.

Then six months later, our "kitten" had three little babies. They looked, ironically, like tiny baby mice squirreling around in the hay by the calves. I quickly rescued them before they drowned in slobber (the calves start producing saliva at the very sight of me).

KitKat appeared and hid her babies away. She seemed a bit offended that I had touched them and no matter how many times I followed her, I never discovered their whereabouts.

One day my husband came into the house. "Found a kitten," he said, "whining in the rain by the shop. I put her in the barn."

No wonder I hadn't found them! She had escaped the barn all together and moved across the driveway to the shop where there is less traffic.

I went out to the barn and found the tiniest little gray kitten curled up on our newest jersey calf. I snuggled her and, for a few minutes, didn't mind cats quite so much.

I went on a hunt at the shop and found two more tiny kittens. One was pitch-black and the other was gray and white. I picked them up and laughed. The black one was a bit bigger than our gray runt but the gray and white one was round as round as could be.

I dubbed her Butterball.

Within three weeks the gray runt and the black kitten had met their end. One under the foot of a cow, the other under the belly of a calf. Butterball, however, stuck around.

In fact, over time, she got quite annoying.

I was quickly remembering why I disliked cats.

This morning was like most mornings. I tripped over her coming out of the milk house. I told her shush when she meowed at me because the first bucket I brought out had wash water instead of milk.

She followed right on my heels as I moved milking units.

Then, when my husband came to help she latched onto his leg to climb to his shoulder. He yelped. Claws got him on his knee.

She jumped from his shoulder to mine and immediately began trying to get her head under my hat.

I tossed her down and got pails of milk for the calves. She nearly jumped out of her skin in excitement and trotted off toward the other end of the barn. I followed her.

When I left the barn she was happily licking up the milk from the bucket she had tipped over.

This evening, however, I noticed she wasn't there when I started milking. In fact, she didn't show up through all of milking. My husband shook his head. "Probably went out of the barn and got hit by a car."

It was sad.

I kind of missed that little bugger.

I was walking toward the milk house, contemplating an interesting Facebook status update about the death of my kitten, when something latched onto my leg.

I still don't like cats. Not really. They're quite gross. I mean, her feet were cold and wet on my neck. Do you realize all the places she might have been? Ilck.

But I kissed her nose anyway.

The Thing About Farm Animals

You might be a dairy farmer if...
you have ever had a constipated
dog or cat because they ate
the used milk filters.
                              - Ken Siegrist

Most farms have more than just cows. It happens, even if you don't mean to let it.

When my mom was a teenager, she wanted a horse something fierce. Grandpa had cows, not horses. He drove tractors, not teams. And he did it on purpose.

Horses are finicky animals. They can overeat and founder, killing themselves. They need to be ridden, brushed, interacted with. You have to be careful what hay you feed them because if it's moldy, they'll eat anyway.

But Mama was the only girl. And the youngest of seven. She sweetly begged until Grandpa could hardly stand another moment. Finally, he found a solution. He would say yes, but with certain stipulations. Conditions that could never be met. He was so pleased with his idea, he practically rubbed his hands together.

"Okay," he told her that night, "you can get a horse *if* you find one that is calm, comes with a saddle and bridle, and costs less than $300." Even back then that price was ridiculously low. Grandpa was certain she'd never find one, but Mama was delighted. She squealed in glee and hugged him tight.

Imagine his surprise when she came running to him the next day. "Come, Daddy," she said, "we need to go look at this horse."

"What?" he asked, thoroughly confused.

"This horse," she explained, showing him the newspaper article with the advertisement.

Long story short? The only-cow farm soon housed a beautiful chestnut quarterhorse named

Capacheno. One that came with a saddle and bridle for less than $300.

That's just how it happens.

You might be a Dairy Farmer if...

strange vehicles are known to stop
at your barn and drop off cats.

On our farm we have cows. And pigs. And cats. And a donkey. And a dog.

Animals just multiply that way.

Kind of like the year my husband's family decided to get rid of their rabbits. They had two (or was it four?) rabbits that were simply not thriving. It seemed like they were always on the brink of death, so the family decided to let them go. They assumed the creatures would go off in the woods to die, but of course, anyone who knows anything about rabbits can guess what happened.

By the next year there were over a hundred (or at least sixty) wild rabbits running around the place, eating the garden, hanging out in the yard.

That's just the way that rabbits are.

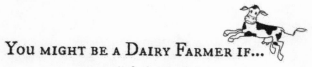

You might be a Dairy Farmer if...

your son's first words are
"tractor," "cow," and "moo."

- Janet Haldeman

Farm animals do have a knack for adding a bit of character to the place.

Our pig pen isn't very big but it comfortably holds two pigs without any trouble. When you add a third pig to the mix, they can get a little pushy. One morning I went out to start milking and there was the piglet, hanging out in the manger. We'd put him back and next thing he'd be out again, having climbed over the backs of his siblings.

When nice weather arrived, the piglet, who by this time was fast friends with the donkey, moved outside. He was a free-range pig, completely by accident.

In fact, at this point we had a regular Old MacDonald farm in our pasture. A free-martin heifer we were raising for beef, the donkey, and Piggly-wiggly himself.

People would stop to take pictures and the animals would all come trotting over, hoping to find some fresh grass or carrots. They were friendly and allowed anyone to pet them.

One day the vet and a farrier, who shoes horses, came to work on Donkey's hooves. We had to get both to come because Donkey has a nice, mule-sized dose of stubborn in him. After several attempts by one and the other, we created a plan of attack that included tranquilizers and three strong men.

"Can you get him in the barn?" the vet asked. I thought so. After all, he came running often enough.

But Donkey smelled a rat and he wouldn't move a muscle. Not one. single. step.

I tried riding him. I tried bribing him. I alternated between sweet-talking and demanding. I dangled carrots in front of his nose. He just stood there.

I finally sat down on the ground a few feet in front of him and whined. "Donkey, this is ridiculous. I should just give your carrots to somebody else." Immediately, I heard a snort next to my left elbow. There was Piggy, the big-lumbering-oversized pet. His beady little eyes were glued on the bag of carrots in my hand.

I offered him one, he wolfed it down, and just like that, Donkey was leaning over me, nosing the carrot bag.

By the time we got to the barn, I was alternating feeding carrots to the pig, the donkey, and the heifer. The vet and the farrier were standing there, shaking their heads. I told them, "You do what you got to do."

Their only suggestion was that I might want to buy stock in carrots.

YOU MIGHT BE A DAIRY FARMER IF...
you've ever spent hours trying to
sweet-talk a four-legged creature
back into the barn.

Donkey isn't the only pet with personality quirks. When my husband was young his family had a dog named Fritz. He was a border collie that their Uncle Harry had found tangled in some fencing on the edge of his farm.

Fritz was a smart dog. A very smart dog.

In fact, there weren't any doors that he couldn't open. The family had planned for him to be a barn dog, but he knew he was above that. He would just open and close any door that stood in his way. The woodshed door, the barn door, even the house door on occasion.

Actually, he was pretty good about staying out of the house. He knew he was a dog, he just wasn't a lowly barn dog. But there was an occasion when he thought that he should be able to find shelter in the house. Every time a thunderstorm came they would find him curled up inside with the family, the door shut behind him.

Amos's family was also given a goat when he was growing up. The day they picked Miss Molly up, they stopped by a neighbor's house before going home.

When they all jumped out of the truck to go inside, she followed them. Their neighbor, a gruff-talking but really-pretty-gentle-underneath type, stood at the door with arms crossed. "Don't bring that goat in here," Mac said, "it'll crap all over my floor."

"Oh, no," the boys told him, "she's a good goat. She goes everywhere with us."

Miss Molly pranced right into his kitchen and the moment she stepped over the threshold, she lifted her tail and began dropping pellets. Mac started hollering and she started running. He grabbed a broom and dustpan and chased that animal through the whole house. The boys would have helped but, well, they were too busy laughing.

Awhile later Mac came to visit the family. He still held a bit of a grudge against Molly so, thinking it would bother her, he gave the goat some of his chewing tobacco.

Wouldn't you know it? That accursed goat ate all the tobacco he had, container and all. Just goes to show you that you can never win against a goat.

You might be a Dairy Farmer if...
you've ever gone on a "kitten hunt" in the hay mow.

My husband's family had more than an extra-smart dog and a tobacco-addicted goat. They also had a pony, a few heifers, a couple geese, and two pigs.

During the winter months the animals would be shut up in the barn, which was a great plan though impossible to actually enforce considering the fact that Fritz could open the barn doors.

The neighbors had a couple horses that Pony enjoyed going to visit. The minute the door opened, out he'd trot. But it didn't stop at that. The heifers were quite fond of their equine friend and would follow him. The goats, hoping for a bit of a snack, and the geese, looking for someone to terrorize, would meander after the heifers. Last of all would come the two lumbering pigs, loath to miss out on any excitement.

Every day they would make the trek down the road to the neighbors and every day my mother-in-law would look out her window, sigh a bit, go to the front door, and call for the pony to come back.

He was a good little pony and would obediently turn and trot back to the barn, the entire parade of creatures following him down the road.

It was all fine and dandy until the day that my in-laws went on vacation. They left an 80-year-old aunt, Emily, to watch the kids and forgot to warn her about the afternoon animal exercise routine.

While the kids were all gone to school, she was quietly cleaning the house when she happened to glance up and saw all the animals, loose and wandering about at will. Being a good-humored and resourceful woman, she immediately went to chase the creatures back into the barn.

The pony, the heifers, the goats, and the geese all understood what she wanted and dutifully wandered back into their prospective homes.

The pigs? Well, pigs are pigs you see.

They thought she was playing a game.

All afternoon she chased those miserable hogs in circles as they squealed and trotted around, finding great enjoyment out of the whole ordeal.

Finally, in exasperation, she gave up and headed for the house. Imagine her surprise when she stepped inside and the pigs, who were distraught to see their entertainment leaving, pushed in right behind her.

With that, the chase was on again.

When the children arrived home from school, they watched in amazement as their almost-always-good-humored aunt began to rant and rave and demand that they do something to help her. "We are not heathens!" she told them with some intensity. "We will not have pigs inside the house!"

One of the children finally said, calm as could be, "All you have to do is call them by name, Aunt Emily."

"What?" she panted.

"Just call them by name," the boys explained, "watch."

They called the pigs, who quick as a lick turned and went lumbering off to the barn. They were rather tired of that game anyway.

YOU MIGHT BE A DAIRY FARMER IF...

you know the difference between hay and straw,
between first, second, third, and fourth cuttings,
and between corn silage and hay silage.

- Ken Siegrist

Extra animals are actually quite handy to have around, despite their shenanigans. We learned this a few months after our donkey moved to the barn.

That year we had a big red and white Holstein bull to breed our cows. We got him when he was quite young but time had been good to him. The muscles were cording on his shoulders and his attitude was growing right along with 'em.

"Don't go into the barn without me," my husband instructed me. "I just don't trust the bull. We need him to cover this next batch of heifers but after that we'll sell him for sure."

One evening the two-thousand-pound animal refused to come in the barn. Instead, he stood in the barnyard pawing at the ground. "I shouldn't have pushed it," Amos said, shaking his head and keeping a tight grip on the pitchfork. "We should have just shipped him and held the heifers off until we found another, younger bull."

Right then I yelped as Donkey shot past me and trotted out to the barnyard. The two males had been threatening each other all week. Donkey would bray and threaten to kick on one side of the fence and the bull would paw at the ground and shake his head, making his nose ring and chain clatter on the other side. "Donkey!" I yelled, reaching to grab at his halter.

He was on a mission and easily slipped past me. The two circled each other in the barn yard, the massive bull and the short little donkey.

"This is going to be bad," Amos said with a moan. I turned my head away but he watched and slowly started to laugh. "You've got to see this," he said, dragging me over to the window.

There was the bull, standing in the middle of the barnyard, swinging his head back and forth, grunting, and pawing the ground, totally confused as Donkey pranced around him, alternating between kicking his nose and biting his shoulder.

The war-dance went on for about fifteen minutes. When they were done, Donkey stood there and watched as the bull tucked his tail and scurried into the barn to his stall. Donkey followed along behind, completely at ease, barely even breathing hard. He stood quietly behind the bull while Amos hooked the neck chain and then disappeared to eat some hay.

The chain of authority was established and never again did the bull give us trouble. Oh, once in awhile he'd get a little sassy but all we had to do was call for Donkey. As soon as he trotted into view the bull would quiet right down and quick as a whistle disappear into his stall.

"The donkey has officially earned his keep," my husband announced.

Of course, the more animals you have, the more time they demand.

I like to accomplish things while I'm waiting to change the milking units, so I keep barn notebooks and write chapters of books on manure splattered pages. Except sometimes Donkey gets annoyed by this practice. He's pretty sure that he is more important than anything I could ever be writing, so the moment my head is bent and the pencil is moving, he will be standing beside me.

Well, he doesn't just stand beside me. He leans. Hard. As in, a shoulder-into-my-back, all-of-his-weight-pushing-on-me type lean. And then before I know it I will have a pig snorting around my feet, a kitten trying to tuck his head under my hat and a puppy dog bouncing three feet in the air trying to get my attention.

It's like they know I keep carrots and beef sticks in my pockets.

The Days I Love the Most

We're cutting back the fence-row, trying to gain room for six extra rows of corn next year. The field that once grew brilliant purple alfalfa has reverted to weeds. We will plow it this spring and plant corn for two years. After that, hopefully we will be able to replant alfalfa.

I am piling thorn-apple logs onto the back of the truck when he says it, "These are the days that I love farming the most."

I smile. Yes. With wind in my hair, piles of wood at my feet and my husband and I spending time together.

To farm is to be close to earth and dirt, sawdust and animals. It means working until you are ready to fall over and breathing in deeply the scent of rain. It means sweat, laughter and nights without sleep. And wind kissing my skin on a perfect autumn day in the old alfalfa field.

As I finish the logs and begin piling the twigs and small branches, I feel a slight squeeze of pain. I thought that by now I would have a three-year-old running around my feet. That I would be teaching a little one to gather sticks for cold winter days.

My plans included having sawdust wars with laughing toddlers and mixing up hot chocolate in sippy-cups.

Plans are such interesting things. You make them and you strive to go after them but sometimes they remain beyond your reach.

Many are the plans in a person's heart, but it is the Lord's purpose that prevails. Proverbs 19:21.

God's ways don't always make sense to me. Infertility has snatched so many hopes away but I am learning to rejoice in the gifts I do have. Like a husband who looks at me with a twinkle in his eye and spins me in bear hugs and kisses me senseless.

Like the earth and the sawdust and the sweat damp on my face. And if sometimes tears add to the dampness, it does not have to ruin a day or snatch the joy from me. For I make so many plans... but it is the Lord's purpose that prevails.

Sometimes it may feel like defeat because I can't force what I want. I can't make things go my way. But always, always it is a promise.

That no matter what. No matter the pain. No matter the tears. No matter the plans that work or don't work, God's purpose prevails.

I think of it later when the stars and moon are shrouded by clouds. Sounds of a banjo playing leak from the barn. It's Sunday night now. The classical station reverts to fiddles and steel guitars late in the evening and my husband smiles. "The cows make more milk on bluegrass," he says.

I step from the barn and a few stray sprinkles of rain dance across my skin. They are cool. I smile into darkness.

The music behind, the glow of the lamp in my kitchen window ahead. My steps slow and I enjoy the breeze that keeps the windmills of Tug Hill turning year-round.

My smile widens. The fields are glittering.

The darkness creates a symphony of sparkles that spin gold into hay fields.

I wish for a way to capture such beauty with a camera lens but it's impossible. Fire-flies are a beauty of the naked eye. Nothing can reconstruct the dance. The gold loses its value without depth and glitter.

I stand and breathe deep. My face is wet now. Raindrops slipping from the end of my nose. My whisper blends with the twang of the banjo and disappears into the twinkle of the gold speckled fields.

"For since the creation of the world God's invisible qualities—his eternal power and divine nature—have been clearly seen, being understood from what has been made, so that men are without excuse." Romans 1:20

God is good. Always, always good. Even when He does not save me from pain. Even when my plans crumble into dust.

I stand, face dripping wet and heart full, breathing deep of earth and life. These are the days, when I'm facing the depth of who God is, when I am face to face with the beauty and goodness that He has created, these are the days that I love the most.

The End of Maple Sugaring

The boys get home and clomp into the house. "We're going to the woods," I tell them before they can pull their shoes off.

"We're going crazy in the woods?" Dominic asks with a grin. He's teasing me as I tease him every day after school.

"When are my mom or dad picking me up?" he *would ask as he dropped his book bag on the floor and pulled his shoes off.*

"Not sure," I usually replied.

"What are we going to do today?" he continues.

"We're going crazy in the woods," I tell him in *mock seriousness.*

"No, really, *Tasha,* really."

"Okay," I wink, *"we're going* really *crazy in the woods."*

Crazy or not, today we step into the pick-up truck. The red one with four-doors. The "car-truck" as my husband says. After car seats are buckled we drive to the barn to pick him up. He's working on a tractor. A Case 1030, his newest project.

I remember when we were first married and tractor numbers would mush together like split-pea soup. 1030, 2640, 4490, 4210… meaningless. I'd give my poor husband a bewildered look then whisper, *"What color is it?"*

It's an International 784 (*it's red*) that takes us out into the woods. It pulls a wagon behind it and I sit there in my hoodie, with jeans tucked into muck-boots and a firm grip on two boys. They are all wide-eyes and laughter as we bump over last year's corn stubs.

Then we're pulling down sap buckets and tripping through underbrush.

"Where's the syrup?" Dominic asks.

"In the sugar shanty by the house," I explain.

"But why are we dumping this syrup?" He points to the yellow sap in the bucket still hooked to the tree.

"This sap isn't good anymore. Look at the trees," I point up and we both stare skyward, "see the green?"

He nods.

"The tree is budding out and that means sugaring is done for the year." Another year of steamy evenings and maple taffy and sap-boiled hotdogs finished.

Later the boys are racing through the maples and leaves are rustling under their feet. I feel my husband's arm slip around me. "Sure is more fun doing the daily things with kids around," he comments.

We watch the littlest one take a face plant. We wait for a cry but he lifts his head, looks at me, and giggles. I blow him kisses.

We're laughing and the grip around my waist tightens. "Thank you, Lord," the deepness of his voice settles in the forest, "that today we get to share our lives with these children."

And I agree with him in prayer. And God is there, under the maple trees, with spring around the corner and joyful giggles bouncing off sap buckets.

The Thing About Farm Kids

You might be a dairy farmer if...
you've ever told your children,
"No, you may not have a horse,
but you may ride the calves."
                            -Dixie Lehman

Kids that grow up on farms have a distinct advantage over those who do not. To begin with, they learn problem solving skills at a very young age. Take for example, my nephew.

Eric's job was to gather eggs each morning. This involved locating a basket, bowl, or bucket and walking the hundred yards to the barn. There he had to slip into the chicken coup and transfer the eggs from the nests to his container.

Sounds simple, but there was one major issue with executing the plan. These were not pet chickens, nor free-range chickens. These were wild chickens. Very wild. And they were ruled by a big rooster who strutted around the coup like he was King Tut. He was nasty and Eric was getting more and more afraid of him.

So, being the excellent problem solver that his parents raised him to be, he looked around for a solution.

Like most farming families, Eric was not an only child. He, in fact, had twin sisters. Aurora, the older of the twins, was always in competition with him. Enlisting her aide was akin to admitting defeat for all eternity. Giselle, on the other hand, was the baby of the family. She often looked at her older brother with admiration. Not only that, but she had an unmistakable gift with animals.

With promises to allow her to play with some of his toys, he bravely and gallantly sent his baby sister into the coup ahead of him to subdue the rooster.

It was an ingenious plan. Giselle loved all animals but had a very definite line of authority. She walked confidently into the chicken coup and told the rooster what-for. When he reacted with a violent peck toward her foot, she flew into a rage and lectured him into submission with flailing arms and loud screeches.

Eric, grinning at his success, walked happily into the coup and gathered his eggs.

It wasn't until later that his plan backfired. His mother happened upon Giselle in the bathroom trying to clean up the blood from a peck to her leg.

"Where did you get that?" she questioned.

"Oh, the rooster did it," Giselle explained.

"Why were you in the chicken coup? Haven't I told you not to play in there?"

"I wasn't playing, Mama, I was just helping Eric."

"Well, Giselle, the eggs are Eric's job. You have your own jobs to do."

A few minutes later Mama found Eric playing in the garden and peppered him with questions.

Thankfully, I arrived for a visit just in time to witness the final display, where she threw her hands in the air and said in exasperation, "You sent your THREE-YEAR-OLD SISTER into the chicken coup to save you from the rooster?"

Eric calmly replied, "Well, it worked, Mom."

In the end, the rooster found its way into the cooking pot, which was the biggest mistake of all. The grisly old thing was so skinny it looked like they had a de-feathered flamingo in the crock pot. No one was really hungry that night.

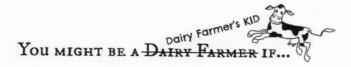

You might be a ~~Dairy Farmer~~ Dairy Farmer's KID if...

you learned drive at the age of 12.

- Tim Lehman

There are more things that just roosters to worry moms on a farm. In fact, why stress about a little feathered creature when there are so many other great things to threaten your babies?

When my mother was a little girl, they would, on occasion, cook up a great delicacy, frog legs. Of course, to eat frog legs, one must go to the frog pond and catch them.

One day my mother, who was just a little tyke, seven or eight years old, decided to go frog catching with some friends and her older brothers. What Mama didn't know, however, was that the men had decided to after-feed the nearby field after the last cutting of hay, and they needed access to the frog pond so the cows could drink.

She was merrily wandering around the pond, up to her waist in muddy water, when she spotted a great big bull frog. It takes some skill to catch a frog, of course, so she proceeded carefully. At the perfect instant she pounced, swiping her hand swiftly toward the creature.

What she caught was the wire to an electric fence, strung through the pond. It was turned up good and hot, since the cows weren't used to the boundaries in this particular area, and Mama was standing waist deep in water.

She started screaming, her hand locked onto the fence. She did what anyone would do, reached her other hand over to free the one that was pulsing electricity through her body. This never works, and instead of having one hand gripping the cursed fence, she now had two.

Her older brothers were watching by now, a bit fascinated with the way she was jerking and screaming that blood-curdling scream.

Her body finally jerked one last time and an electric arch sent her flying backwards, dunking her entire body into the silt and mud of the pond. She was unhurt, thankfully, but madder than a soaking wet Tom cat.

You would think that after all this her brothers would be rushing to rescue their baby sister, and perhaps they would have if she had been seriously injured. But alas, she stood to her feet spewing pond water and they laughed so hard they were rolling on the ground in glee.

Still, even with the potential seriousness of this experience, Mama learned at a relatively young age, a very important lesson. You don't stand in water and touch an electric fence. Ever. Even by accident.

And her brothers learned an important lesson as well. A screaming little sister is not something to laugh at, unless you want to be pummeled.

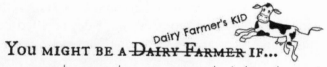

YOU MIGHT BE A ~~DAIRY FARMER~~ Dairy Farmer's KID IF...
you always take someone else's hand
before you grab the electric fence.
- Ken Siegrist

There is something about growing up on a farm that make kids tough. It doesn't even have to be a dairy farm. Just living out in the country without constant overprotective parental supervision will do it.

Our society today has tried to protect kids to such an extent that they grow up a bit on the clueless side. Living on a farm makes that impossible. There are too many things to do besides watch the kids and yell if they start to do something dangerous. You just have to trust that they'll figure it out.

Take, for instance, the day my dad was in the barn and saw a calf stealing milk out of a pail.

He was quick and resourceful, so when the calf didn't respond to his voice command, he grabbed a baseball bat and knocked her over the head. She, promptly, stopped drinking.

The problem being, the reason she stopped was because she was too busy dying.

Yup. Fell right over dead as a doornail.

Now, if his mother had been standing right beside him, she may have been able to prevent this traumatic event but the lesson would not have run nearly as deep.

When I hear of extremely violent young people I often think of Papa telling us the story of the dead calf, his face still a bit ashen even as an adult. He never intended to kill the thing, or even to seriously hurt it, so a very real distaste for violence settled in. In fact, I've always thought of him as a very gentle man.

See, farms make smart kids which translate into great adults.

YOU MIGHT BE A ~~DAIRY FARMER~~ IF... Dairy Farmer's KID
you had corn cob fights with your siblings during chores.

- Ken Siegrist

When your children are too small to leave your side, you do a lot of talking and pray that some common sense will leak into their blood stream. "Don't touch bright colored reptiles," you explain, secretly hoping that they never touch any, ever. Yet, you know somehow, deep down, that they will. So you warn them about the poisonous ones and prepare yourself for the inevitable.

Like the day Giselle brought the garden snake onto the porch to show us all. She had learned to be careful and catch them behind the head, since even non-poisonous snakes *can* bite.

There is was, dangling from her fingers, her face displaying her pride at the obvious brilliance she had utilized to catch it. "Do you want to pet it?" she asked her little cousins. They were amenable to the idea and the mamas and aunts tried to restrain their natural tendency to say no and protect all the children from the slimy creature.

Everything was going fine until the moment when the baby caught sight of it. At ten months he was quite adept at grabbing onto toys and this seemed like the greatest of all playthings. He reached forward from his mama's lap and wrapped his little hand right around the squirming reptile.

Giselle was quite taken by surprise but kept her grip on the now angry snake. Unfortunately, the baby was not about to let go of his new toy. His mama was working franticly to peel his little fingers away when suddenly Giselle lost control.

Mayhem followed. The snake went flying, mamas grabbed children, kids screamed (or was that the adults?), people scrambled up onto chairs. Over the din of the noise, Giselle's mother could be heard, her voice deadly serious, "Get that snake out of my house right this minute. Right this very minute, Giselle. Get it out of here."

Her snake catching abilities tripled with her mother's voice prompting her and the creature was quickly returned to the wild. The kids were off running and playing a few minutes later and the adults were left sitting on the now-destroyed front porch, taking deep breaths and lifting shaky hands to wipe the sweat from their brows.

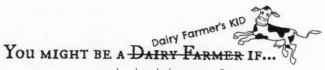

You might be a ~~Dairy Farmer~~ Dairy Farmer's KID if...

you ever built elaborate forts
in the hay mow.

- Erica West

We always knew it was Giselle who had this irresistible draw toward animals. I think I understood that it was a true gift the first time she ever milked a cow.

The twins were visiting that evening around chore time and begged to come to the barn with us. Aurora was content to just watch, but Giselle was determined to help me milk. She was only five years old but was quite capable of making her desires known.

I brought her into the stall with me and squatted down to place the milker on the cow. I kept her standing safely between my legs and explained how to hold the milking unit. The cow, who was almost-always perfectly calm and collected, decided to kick. Of course. I swiftly pulled Giselle back into my arms to shield her from the flying hoof.

"Whoa," I said, pinching the skin between the cow's leg and udder, "hold still." Giselle was quiet, so we went ahead and put the milker on without any issue. As we stood up I laughed. "Good thing she didn't get you, huh?"

Giselle turned slowly, her face coming into view with a huge streak of manure across it, and said with quiet dignity, "Actually, she kind of did."

It didn't stop her though. By the end of the evening, she was putting on the milking units herself and was quite adept at making the cows mind.

Lecturing animals must run in the family.

YOU MIGHT BE A ~~DAIRY FARMER~~ Dairy Farmer's KID IF...
you've ever followed along behind the plow
to hunt for fishing worms.
- Stephanie Schwartz

Of course farm kids are still kids. They still have to learn the regular old lessons of life, like how to sit quietly at school, how to look both ways before crossing the street, and most of all, how to be truthful.

When my grandmother was young she attended the Harrisburg District #2 school. It was a one room schoolhouse where all the grades were together, little ones in the front, older kids in the back, and all the middles in between.

One September day, the teacher, Miss Peck, told the students all about her summer experiences. She had a magazine which she enjoyed reading and she said there was an address where she could send in a drawing of all their hands and they could have their "fortunes" told. She gave each of them a plain sheet of paper and told them to have their fingers all together and the thumb out a little and trace around it, holding the pencil straight up.

Well, Grandma's hands were large. She was always told she had "large and strong Lehman hands" like her father and his relatives. Her mother had small hands and her sister Charlotte did too. She also had a little girl friend, almost a year older than her, who was small as well. The friend always explained that she was delicate and her mother would tell Grandma that too, which she interpreted to mean that she should let her friend do whatever she wanted when they played. Even for meals her friend would have special things to eat sometimes, like cream for her cereal and more butter on her potatoes. Grandma didn't mind that too much, she always felt strong and healthy, but when she thought about having her fortune told she wanted to have the future of a delicate, dainty lady who fainted easily and had a hint of dark circles under her eyes.

Besides that, whoever heard of a heroine in a romantic story dropping a large glove? No, it was always a small glove and Cinderella's glass slipper was little as well. Too tiny for the big, ugly stepsisters!

So Grandma decided to take things into her own hands. Literally.

She scrunched her fingers together and caused her hand to contract as much as possible. She tipped her pencil slightly and drew around her hand under the edge just a smidgen. It really looked like a dainty romantic hand on that sheet!

They didn't hear any more about their fortunes coming back as the weeks went by. It would cross her mind now and then, but she wasn't particularly concerned about it. After all, a lovely romantic future probably wouldn't come about until she was older any way.

All the students had forgotten about it by the time December rolled around. They had so much to do, getting ready for their big, very special, annual Christmas program and party. The whole community would attend, even people in the district who didn't have children in school, and sometimes the children's relatives would come as well.

One of the men would help cut a huge, fifteen-foot Christmas tree and Miss Peck would bring decorations and have the children make paper chains with red and green construction paper. It was quite the celebration.

On this particular year, they had just finished singing one of the carols when the door burst open and there was a loud, "Ho, ho, ho!" A fat jolly Santa Claus came in and shook hands with all the people. Afterward he stood by the blackboard and handed out gifts.

All the children received beautiful hand-knitted mittens. Grandma's were a lovely variegated green made special for a dainty little hand—much too small for her.

In fact, they were too small for her sister Charlotte as well and had to be passed on to one of her little brothers.

Her "fortune" was obvious: If you lie about the size of your hands, you'll end up with mittens that don't fit.

YOU MIGHT BE A ~~DAIRY FARMER~~ Dairy Farmer's KID IF...

you walk barefoot in the pasture
and don't care what you step in.

- Jennifer Metzler

The best part of raising kids on a farm is not just the inevitable lessons they will learn but also the chances you will have to build memories with them because you're working together, all at the same location. This opens the door for so many great opportunities to share life. You just have to get a little creative.

Like the story about the time my Uncle Loren's wagon got stuck. He was just a little boy and his red express wagon that he tried to pull through a puddle was up past the wheels in mud.

In tears he went to his father. Grandpa, who probably had a few dozen things on his list to accomplish that day, went to investigate the problem. He walked around the puddle, looking at the forlorn little wagon and shaking his head gravely. "It's really stuck, son," he told him, "really stuck."

After a bit of debate, he pulled one of the best father-becomes-superman stunts of all time. "Hold on, boy," he told his son, "let me get the tractor. We'll get your wagon out if it's the last thing we do."

The big tractor was chained to the wagon, the boys were told to stand back, the engine was revved, and just for effect Grandpa popped the clutch and stalled. "It sure is stuck!" he hollered over his shoulder. "But we'll get'er yet." After a bit more engine rumbling and jerking on the chain, the little wagon finally made it to solid ground.

And on that day, a wagon was saved and a memory was made and all those things that Grandpa needed to accomplish? We don't even know what they were. All we know is that Grandpa was superman and he saved the wagon and the day and he loved his children well.

Grandpa and Uncle Loren saving the express wagon

Growing up on a farm gives kids the perfect opportunity to learn how to build families. To create memories. And to learn to identify the real and lasting things over foolish pursuits.

And, of course, to let them grow up smart. The kind of smart that's earned by experience.

Before Winter

The sun had long been set as we step from the warmth of the barn into the cool of the night. His hand slips into mine as we climb the hill toward the house. He tugs gently and my feet leave the rough rocks of the driveway and slide onto cool grass.

"Come on a ride with me," he whispers into the evening air, "it's such a nice night. It might be the last one before winter, you know."

I'm fighting exhaustion. Every scrap of daylight was spent in the fields. His eyes entreat me in the moonlight.

I step onto the four-wheeler and wait for him to settle in front of me. My arms wrap tight around him and I rest my head on his back. My jeans and hooded sweatshirt are plenty warm, even on this November evening.

The sound of the engine is loud in the quiet. I press myself against him, watching as the ground flashes by. The faded hay fields are dormant, ready for snow. The oat field cut, and a pile of oats and bales of straw fill the barn. The winter wheat dug deep in moist soil.

We stop under the closest windmill. It's whistling in the breeze, swishing its way downward then whirling back up. I watch the identical silhouettes that dot the hillside, turning softly in the unrelenting Tug Hill breeze.

Grandma said it, long ago, "Tug Hill will rise again." She'd laugh and her soft hands would fold peacefully. They farmed for years on the plateau, back when the land was shrugged off as worthless because of too much snow, too many hills, too little sunlight, too much wind. They scratched out a living and she would shake her head and say, even after they retired and moved to town, "It's good land up there."

Then the windmills came that filled the countryside and put cash into farmer's pockets. They rise majestically on the horizon, towering over the hay fields filled with fine grasses that feed the cows all winter long.

The land my husband bought on a dream and a gamble pays him back month after month.

We leave the windmill and I think we are going back home but he passes the house and heads across the highway. We slip behind the barn and into the back fields. Two deer jump out in front of us, startled by our sudden appearance. They bound across the path and disappear into the corn, their white tails winking goodbye. We laugh under stars.

The corn looks scant in some places. Deer have eaten their fill and there is evidence that a bear tromped through the back corner.

"We'll hopefully get this in tomorrow," he waves his hand at the corn, with ears bending low. I try to focus on his words, but I am a bit apprehensive at the thought of a black bear jumping in front of us.

He stops the wheeler and picks an ear of corn. It is full and dented. Perfect. I grip it in my hand as we turn back toward the house. I see the kitchen light glowing warm and soft across the fields.

We pull up beside my red pick-up truck, the bed full of yellow cobs from the field by the windmill road. The ear from my hand disappears into the corn pile. The pigs will be happy.

The moonlight still calls so we ride the fence-line, checking the apple trees to make sure they are picked clean. A single golden apple is snagged from the branch. It is sweet and soft from frost. I wipe the juice from my chin.

The towering maples are bare of leaves. We talk about where to put our sugar shanty that we are building for spring. It will be small. Our two-by-six evaporator doesn't require much room. I can almost smell the sticky sweetness as his voice speaks dreams in the stillness. I can picture the rows of canning jars filled with amber liquid. There will be laughter, hotdogs, late nights, and cups of fresh syrup.

Spring is still far off. First there will be months of cold and snow that glitters across wide-open fields. There will cups of coffee wrapped in cold hands and days of thankfulness for four-wheel drive vehicles. Months will pass where the animals will stand in their stalls and eat hay that was sundried on windy summer days. There will be evenings of popcorn and woodstoves glowing red.

He shifts and we skim over the ground, through the fallow field where the brown grass is glowing gold in starlight. I tilt my head and stare at the heavens. There are no clouds. It is glorious. Beauty that could only be created by a God who delights in blessing.

I can smell winter, that bite in the air that promises the end of this Indian summer. It crackles in the clear sky with the low draping stars that pale in comparison to the three-quarters moon that graces the tree line.

When we finally pull into the front yard, I am barely awake. My head is resting on his back and I blink when the engine is cut and pure quiet settles. We still and breathe and I hear his heart beating under my cheek.

The silence breaks as the milk truck downshifts and pulls into the driveway. We stay quiet and listen as a few thousand pounds of milk are pumped from our tank. It will be a month until we see the money from our labor but I smile anyway.

We step from the wheeler and I brush strands of hair out of my eyes. He takes my hand and pulls me close for a moment longer. I glory that he chose to marry me and share this life.

"Thanks," he whispers into my hair, "thanks for riding with me."

My smile deepens. "It was beautiful," I answer, my voice heavy with sleep, "maybe the last one before winter."

ACKNOWLEDGMENTS

It would have been impossible to write a book about farming if my husband hadn't been willing to actually fill the barn with cows. Thank you, dear, for every single day that you stood in the barn with me. I wouldn't trade those years of working together for all the world.

And Meg. This book would have just been an idea strewn across three mobile devices had you not helped me create a plan. Those quiet Alaskan afternoons were plum useful, even if I forgot the planner that was going to change my life.

We cannot forget my sister-in-law, Brianna, and her magical artist pen. Your little sketches inspired me to finish. Thank you. Oh, and thanks for having such entertaining kiddos. They really spiced up the manuscript.

Grandma Polly, who shared stories from her childhood and tales of Grandpa and the farm. I'm so thankful for the heritage you've given me.

To the blog readers who have left me comments and encouraged my writing, thank you. To the gals in my blogging mastermind group who saw the first draft of the front cover and boosted my confidence with their rave reviews, thank you. To the friends who jumped up and down in excitement when I announced another book was in the works, thank you.

Without y'all this would never be.

And before I go can I tell you a little story? I know, I know, I've told plenty of them already, but this one is special.

You see, when I first started this book I had no idea that I would be walking through one of the most difficult seasons of my life. My first book, *Pain Redeemed,* was already written and published and it truly seemed that my "painful moments" were behind me. But of course, that's not how it works.

But God gave me a delicious gift. This book.

See, the last time I went through a summer of trials, my attempts at humor were cynical at best and angry at the worst. But one of the beautiful things about knowing and following God is that He changes us over time. He wears down the rough edges and heals us up.

I know because this time, when life got hard, I wrote a book full of humor. And it's not angry or cynical at all. It's funny!

Hallelujah! to a God who touches the broken. May you, dear reader, learn to know this loving God for yourself.

ABOUT THE AUTHOR

Natasha Metzler lives with her husband
on a farm in Northern New York.
She blogs at natashametzler.com
and still refuses to spread manure.

You can contact her at
natashametzler@gmail.com

SHARE YOUR FARMING STORIES AND JOKES

Do you know a great farming story or joke?

Come visit
natashametzler.com/dairyfarmerbook
and share!

Made in the USA
Charleston, SC
29 September 2014